Big Machines At Work

Diggers

By Jean Eick

SCHOLASTIC INC.

New York   Toronto   London   Auckland   Sydney
Mexico City   New Delhi   Hong Kong   Buenos Aires

For information regarding permission, write to:
The Child's World®, Inc.
P.O. Box 326
Chanhassen, Minnesota 55317

Photos: © 1998 David M. Budd Photography

ISBN 0-439-65053-4

Printed in the U.S.A.
First Scholastic printing, February 2004

Contents

On the Job

On the job, diggers work at **construction sites.** Diggers are needed to dig big holes for new buildings.

A digger does not move on wheels and tires. It moves on huge **crawler tracks.** These big metal belts spin around to make the digger move forward and backward.

The digger moves so slowly that it cannot drive itself from job to job. Instead, it rides on the back of a big truck.

A digger has a long arm with a giant bucket attached. The bucket has long metal teeth that can tear into the ground. When the digger digs a hole, the long arm reaches down and the bucket scoops up a load of dirt.

Then the arm brings the bucket up.

The whole machine turns around and . . .

Crash, bang! The dirt from the bucket crashes into the box of a dump truck.

Quickly, the digger turns back to the hole.

It must dig and dump until the hole is
big enough for the new building.

Climb Aboard!

Would you like to see where the driver sits? The digger's driver is called the **operator.** The operator uses **pedals** and **levers** to make the machine swing around and move. Special levers called **joysticks** make the big arm move and the bucket dig.

Up Close

The inside

1. The operator's seat

2. The pedals and levers

3. The joysticks

The outside

1. The crawler tracks

2. The arm

3. The bucket

Glossary

construction sites (kun-STRUCK-shun SITES)
Construction sites are places where something is being built.
Diggers dig big holes for new buildings at construction sites.

crawler tracks (KRAWL-er TRAX)
Crawler tracks are huge metal belts that spin around to move
the digger back and forth.

levers (LEV-erz)
Levers are sticks with round knobs on the ends. The operator
uses levers to make the digger swivel and move.

joysticks (JOY-sticks)
Joysticks are similar to the controls for video games. The
operator uses joysticks to move the digger's arm and bucket.

operator (OPP-er-ay-ter)
The operator is the person who drives the digger and uses the
controls that make the digger work.

pedals (PED-elz)
Pedals are controls that people work with their feet. The operator
uses pedals to make the digger move.